A *is for* Angel
The Alphabet in Sacred Art

Adrienne Keogler, Katie Keogler, and Jaimee Keogler

Get Creative 6

Through Our Lady, we dedicate this book to
Paul A. Muhs, in gratitude for the countless hours
he read to us, his children, grandchildren,
and great-grandchildren.

Saint Joachim and Saint Anne, good parents of the
Blessed Virgin Mary, grandparents of our Savior,
Jesus Christ, *pray for us.*

Get Creative 6
An imprint of Mixed Media Resources
104 West 27th Street
Third Floor
New York, NY 10001

Connect with us on Facebook at
facebook.com/getcreative6

Senior Editor
MICHELLE BREDESON

Art Director
IRENE LEDWITH

Chief Executive Officer
CAROLINE KILMER

President
ART JOINNIDES

Chairman
JAY STEIN

Copyright © 2020 by Keogler Books LLC

All rights reserved. No part of this publication may be reproduced or used in any form or by any means—graphic, electronic, or mechanical, including photocopying, recording, or information storage-and-retrieval systems—without permission of the publisher.

Library of Congress Cataloging-in-Publication Data available upon request.

978-1-68462-011-1

Manufactured in the United States of America

3 5 7 9 10 8 6 4

First Edition

A Note to Readers

Beauty, like truth, brings joy to the human heart and is that precious fruit which resists the erosion of time, which unites generations and enables them to be one in admiration!" —The Council Fathers Message to Artists (December 8, 1965)

Welcome to our petite treasury of sacred art! Our intention with this book is to immerse little ones, and not so little ones, into the world of sacred art and open them up to the beauty of our faith. Are children capable of appreciating such "grown-up" works of art? Absolutely! Children are amazingly open to true beauty in all its forms. With your guidance, they will learn to see the mark of God in all created things, including great works of art. There are several ways you can enjoy this book with a child:

- Simply gaze upon each work of art, asking them to find small details in the piece as you notice them, or ask the child their thoughts and feelings about the work. This will help the child sink deeply into the work of art and dwell there for a while. It is a very peaceful exercise.

- Read the rhyming text that accompanies each picture to provide rich lessons for children and serve as a little "catechism," helping them to remember the truths of the faith.

- Use the text together with the picture to further illuminate the teaching of each letter.

For those who want to delve deeper, the information on each painting, including artist, date, and country of origin is provided to broaden the understanding of the universality of our faith, and how it has influenced great artists through the centuries and throughout the world. Regarding an encounter with a work of art, Pope Benedict stated: "Indeed it resembles a door open on to the infinite, on to a beauty and a truth that go beyond the daily routine. And a work of art can open the eyes of the mind and of the heart, impelling us upward." ■

Angel

Angels adore on bended knee
the Christ Child born to set us free.

Virgin of the Angels • William-Adolphe Bouguereau • 1881

Aa

Bb — Baptism

The water of **Baptism** washes our sin away.

Christening in Assisi • Vicente Poveda • 1899

Creation

God made all of **Creation** where we live, grow, and play.

Cc

The Garden of Eden • Jan Brueghel the Elder • c. 1612

JESUS, I TRUST IN YOU

Divine Mercy

Rays of **Divine Mercy** shine down white and red.

Vilnius Divine Mercy Image • Eugene Kazimirowski • 1934

Eucharist

Jesus in the **Eucharist** is our life-giving bread.

Ee

The Eucharist • artist unknown • 1660

Father

Ff

God is our **Father** in Heaven; we are His joy and delight.

God the Father • Pierre Mignard I • c. 1664

Glory

Angels sang **"Glory to God"** on the very first Christmas night.

Gg

Fresco in Shepherd's Field Chapel • U. Noni • 1953

Hh — Holy Spirit

The **Holy Spirit** is the love between the Father and the Son.

Mosaic of the Holy Spirit • Mauméjean House • 1934

Incense

Prayers are like **incense** rising to The Almighty One.

I i

Queen of the Angels • William-Adolphe Bouguereau • 1900

Jj

Joseph & Jesus

Saint **Joseph** was **Jesus's** father while He lived upon the Earth.

Saint Joseph the Carpenter • Georges de La Tour • c. 1642

King

Christ now reigns in Heaven;
He is **King** of the Universe.

Jesus Christ as King of the World • Karl von Blaas • 19th Century

Ll

Love

Jesus said, "**Love** one another as I have loved you."

Christ on the Road to Emmaus • Jan Wildens • c. 1640s

Mass

At Holy **Mass** we hear God's Word and receive the Eucharist, too.

Mm

Another Christ • Charles Bosseron Chambers • 20th Century

Nativity

In a stable in Bethlehem, was the **Nativity** of Our Lord.

Nativity • Noël-Nicolas Coypel • 1728

Ordained

When a priest is **ordained**,
the grace of Christ is outpoured.

Oo

Ordination and First Mass of St. John of Matha •
Vicente Carducho • c. 1634

Pp Prayer

We open our hearts to God when we kneel down in **prayer**.

The Evening Prayer • Pierre Édouard Frère • 1857

Queen

Mary is the **Queen** of Heaven; she keeps us in her care.

Coronation of the Virgin • Diego Vélazquez • 1635

Resurrection

Rr

At the **Resurrection**, Jesus rose from the grave.

The Resurrection • Joseph Wild and Rudolph Mader • c. 1930

Saint

Our friends in Heaven are the **saints**; they are good, holy, and brave.

Ss

*The Forerunners of Christ with Saints and Martyrs •
Guido di Pietro (Fra Angelico) • c. 1424*

Trinity

Tt

Our God is a **Trinity**: three Persons who are equal.

The Holy Trinity • Giovanni Maria Conti della Camera • c. 1640

Universal

The Church is **universal** because She serves all people.

Interior of the Cathedral of Amiens • Jules Victor Génisson • 1842

Visitation

Vv

At the **Visitation**,
Elizabeth greeted Mary with joyful praise.

Visitation • Carl Bloch • 1866

Water

Jesus walked on **water**;
He calmed the wind and stormy waves.

Christ at the Sea of Galilee • artist unknown • c. 1575

Ww

Xx —Crucifixion—

At the **Crucifixion**,
Jesus died to save us from our sins.

Crucifixion • Prospero Mallerini • 1801

Yes

When Mary said "**Yes**,"
God's plan of salvation could begin.

Annunciation • Guido di Pietro (Fra Angelico) • c. 1445

Zz

–Zeal–

The angels and saints are filled with **zeal**, enjoying their heavenly reward.

Disputation of the Holy Sacrament • Raffaello Sanzio da Urbino (Raphael) • c. 1510

We are called to follow their example
to love and serve the Lord!

Artwork Information

Cover
The Sistine Madonna (1512)
Raffaello Sanzio da Urbino (Raphael) (Italian)
Oil on canvas (detail)
Gemäldegalerie Ale Meister, Dresden, Germany

Aa Angel
Virgin of the Angels (1881)
William-Adolphe Bouguereau (French)
Oil on canvas (detail)
Getty Center, Los Angeles, California

Bb Baptism
Christening in Assisi (1899)
Vicente Poveda (Spanish)
Oil on canvas (detail)
Private collection

Cc Creation
The Garden of Eden (c. 1612)
Jan Brueghel the Elder (Flemish)
Oil on panel (detail)
Thyssen-Bornemisza National Museum, Madrid, Spain

Dd Divine Mercy
Vilnius Divine Mercy Image (1934)
Eugene Kazimirowski (Polish)
Oil on canvas
Divine Mercy Shrine, Vilnius, Lithuania
Used with permission of the Marian Fathers of the Immaculate Conception of the B.V.M.

Ee Eucharist
The Eucharist (1660)
Artist unknown (Spanish)
Oil on canvas
Nationalmuseum, Stockholm, Sweden

Ff Father
God the Father (c. 1664)
Pierre Mignard I (French)
Oil on canvas (detail)
National Gallery of Art, Washington, D.C.

Gg Glory
Fresco in Shepherd's Field Chapel (1953)
U. Noni (Palestinian)
Fresco (detail)
Shepherd's Field Chapel, Bethlehem, Palestine

Hh Holy Spirit
Mosaic of the Holy Spirit (1934)
Mauméjean House (French)
Mosaic (detail)
The Chapel of Our Lady of the Miraculous Medal, Paris, France

Ii Incense
Queen of the Angels (1900)
William-Adolphe Bouguereau (French)
Oil on canvas
Petit Palais, Paris, France

Jj Joseph & Jesus
Saint Joseph the Carpenter (c. 1642)
Georges de La Tour (French)
Oil on canvas (detail)
Louvre Museum, Paris, France

Kk King
Jesus Christ as King of the World (19th Century)
Karl von Blaas (Austrian)
Fresco (detail)
Altlerchenfelder Church, Vienna, Austria

Ll Love
Christ on the Road to Emmaus (c. 1640s)
Jan Wildens (Flemish)
Oil on canvas (detail)
The State Hermitage Museum, St. Petersburg, Russia

Mm Mass
Another Christ (20th Century)
Charles Bosseron Chambers (American)
Charcoal (detail)
Location unknown

Nn Nativity
Nativity (1728)
Noël-Nicolas Coypel (French)
Oil on canvas
The Palace of Versailles, Versailles, France

Oo Ordained
Ordination and First Mass of St. John of Matha (c. 1634)
Vicente Carducho (Italian)
Oil on canvas
Prado Museum, Madrid, Spain

Pp Prayer
The Evening Prayer (1857)
Pierre Édouard Frère (French)
Oil on panel
Rijksmuseum, Amsterdam, Netherlands
Used with permission of Rijksmuseum, Amsterdam

Qq Queen
Coronation of the Virgin (1635)
Diego Velázquez (Spanish)
Oil on canvas (detail)
Prado Museum, Madrid, Spain

Rr Resurrection
The Resurrection (c. 1930)
Joseph Wild & Rudolph Mader (Austrian)
Mosaic (detail)
Church of St. Francis of Assisi, New York, New York
Photo by Anthony Jaladoni

Ss Saint
The Forerunners of Christ with Saints and Martyrs (c. 1424)
Guido di Pietro (Fra Angelico) (Italian)
Egg tempera on wood
National Gallery, London, England

Tt Trinity
The Holy Trinity (c. 1640)
Giovanni Maria Conti della Camera (Italian)
Fresco (detail)
Santa Croce, Parma, Italy

Uu Universal
Interior of the Cathedral of Amiens (1842)
Jules Victor Génisson (Belgian)
Oil on canvas
Pinacoteca do Estado de São Paulo, São Paulo, Brazil

Vv Visitation
Visitation (1866)
Carl Bloch (Flemish)
Oil on copper (detail)
Frederiksborg Museum of Natural History, Copenhagen, Denmark

Ww Water
Christ at the Sea of Galilee (c. 1575)
Unknown artist from the Jacopo Tintoretto circle (Italian)
Oil on canvas
National Gallery of Art, Washington, D.C.

Xx Crucifixion
Crucifixion (1801)
Prospero Mallerini (Italian)
Oil on canvas
National Gallery of Victoria, Melbourne, Australia

Yy Yes
Annunciation (c. 1445)
Guido di Pietro (Fra Angelico) (Italian)
Fresco (detail)
Museo di San Marco, Florence, Italy

Zz Zeal
Disputation of the Holy Sacrament (c. 1510)
Raffaello Sanzio da Urbino (Raphael) (Italian)
Fresco (detail)
Stanza della Segnatura, Vatican City